step-by-step cooking

INDIAN

delightful ideas for everyday meals

step-by-step cooking

INDIAN

delightful ideas for everyday meals

Dhershini Govin Winodan

mc **Marshall Cavendish**
Cuisine

The Publisher wishes to thank Lim's Arts and Living for the loan and use of their tableware.

Photographer: Sam Yeo

First published 2005 as Feast of Flavours from the Indian Kitchen
This new edition 2009

Published by Marshall Cavendish Cuisine
An imprint of Marshall Cavendish International
1 New Industrial Road, Singapore 536196

Other Marshall Cavendish Offices:
Marshall Cavendish Ltd. 5th Floor, 32-38 Saffron Hill, London EC1N 8FH, UK • Marshall Cavendish
Corporation. 99 White Plains Road, Tarrytown NY 10591-9001, USA • Marshall Cavendish International
(Thailand) Co Ltd. 253 Asoke, 12th Flr, Sukhumvit 21 Road, Klongtoey Nua, Wattana, Bangkok 10110,
Thailand • Marshall Cavendish (Malaysia) Sdn Bhd, Times Subang, Lot 46, Subang Hi-Tech Industrial
Park, Batu Tiga, 40000 Shah Alam, Selangor Darul Ehsan, Malaysia.

Marshall Cavendish is a trademark of Times Publishing Limited

National Library Board Singapore Cataloguing in Publication Data

Dhershini Govin Winodan, 1953
Indian : delightful ideas for everyday meals / Dhershini Govin Winodan. New ed. Singapore: Marshall
Cavendish Cuisine, 2009.
p. cm. (Step-by-step cooking series)
ISBN-13 : 978-981-261-798-9
ISBN-10 : 981-261-798-1

1. Cookery, Indic. I. Title. II. Series: Step-by-step cooking series (Marshall Cavendish Cuisine)

TX724.5.I4
641.5954 -- dc22   OCN319670342

Printed in Singapore by Times Printers Pte Ltd

CONTENTS

COOKING TECHNIQUES

KNEADING

Kneading is a technique used in making breads. Once the ingredients have been assembled, use your fingers to gather them together and mix into a smooth, pliable dough. Do this slowly so air is incorporated into the mixture to achieve a light and feathery texture for the final baked product.

When you have a ball of dough, rub a little ghee (clarified butter), olive oil or any cooking oil all over it and place it in a bowl to rest. Cover it with a cloth or some plastic wrap to prevent the dough from drying out.

MARINATING

Like kneading, use your hands when marinating. This way, you will be able to feel it as you rub the sauces and chopped ingredients into the meat or fish. It is best to marinate meats fresh from the market. Clean, then decide on your recipe and marinate the meat accordingly. Pack the marinated meats into zip lock bags, label them and refrigerate for 2–3 hours. This will allow the marinade to infuse the meat. Lastly, place them in the freezer until required. With seafood, however, just freeze them fresh from the market. Clean just before cooking. Cleaning, washing and freezing rob seafood of their natural flavours.

HANDLING SPICES

There are dry and wet spices. Dry spices include chilli powder, coriander, cumin, pepper and turmeric, and these are easily available at the supermarket. Powdered forms of these spices are also available at the supermarket, but as spices do not retain their flavour well, grind them yourself in small batches. Pick out the small stones and sticks that sometimes find their way into the spices and roast in a dry pan over very low heat until the spice is hot to the touch. Leave to cool slightly before grinding in a coffee mill set aside specially for this purpose. Store in a clean, dry jar. Wet spices are generally made only when required with fresh

INTRODUCTION

ingredients. To make, dry-roast the dry spices and grind with a little water.

In Indian cooking, it is always handy to have chilli paste stored up in the refrigerator. You can prepare it by soaking a handful of dried red chillies in boiling water until softened. Drain and put into the blender. Add a few cloves of peeled garlic and a couple of peeled shallots, then grind into a smooth paste. Add a pinch of salt, stir and store in a clean and dry jar. This chilli paste is great for stir-fries and fish curries, and can also be used as a marinade.

BROWNING FOODS

Allowing foods to brown in the pan with or without fat over moderate heat creates greater flavour in the final dish. Allow meats to cook through on one side before flipping over to cook the other side.

Browning onions is a sure way of getting that full-bodied flavour in curries and briyanis. Crisp-fried onions are also great toppings for soups, noodles and even plain rice. To crisp-fry onions, peel, then finely slice. Heat oil until smoking, then add the sliced onions. After a minute, reduce the heat and allow the onions to continue to brown. Drain completely on absorbent paper and store away.

TEMPERING

This is one of my favourite cooking techniques. Some recipes call for two temperings and some just one. In Indian cooking, tempering refers to the process of heating a little oil, adding your aromatics like cinnamon, cardamom and cloves or, in most cases, mustard seeds, curry leaves, onions and chillies. The general idea is to allow the ingredients to release their flavours and fragrance into the oil. This is then added to the main ingredients for the flavour to be absorbed. The second tempering also uses the same ingredients—oil, mustard seeds, curry leaves, sliced onions and sometimes dried red chillies and dhal. These are fried to a golden brown, then poured over the prepared curries and sauces to seal in the flavour.

EXTRACTING JUICES/MILK

In Indian cooking, the extracting of juices/milk refers mainly to coconut milk and tamarind juice. Packets of ready extracted coconut milk are now available from the supermarket, so you don't have to go through the tedious process of extracting the milk from the freshly grated coconut. In some Indian homes, however, the freshly extracted milk is still preferred.

Tamarind juice is not as readily available, but the process is much easier than extracting coconut milk. Take a lime-sized ball of tamarind pulp and place in a small bowl. Add enough water to cover, then knead with your hand until the pulp is separated from the seeds. Strain and discard the seeds. Use the juice according to the recipe.

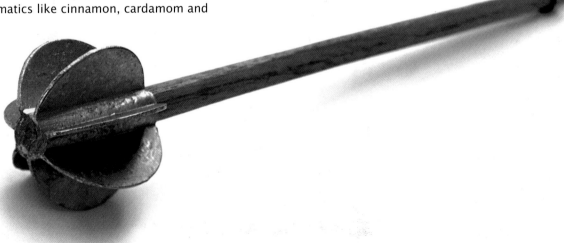

COOKING UTENSILS

CAST IRON WOK

Woks are made from various materials such as aluminium, stainless steel and may sometimes be coated with a non-stick surface. In Indian cooking, cast iron woks are traditionally used. Once seasoned, these cast iron woks can last for years. You can cook almost anything in a cast iron wok, including stir-fries, curries and deep-fried foods.

To season a new cast iron wok, wash it well with soap and water. Wipe it dry, then heat it over a low fire. This is to ensure that the wok is completely dry. Leave the wok to cool, then drizzle some oil into the wok. Use a kitchen towel and rub the oil all over the wok. Keep the oiled wok away in a dry bag for a day and repeat the oiling process at least three times. Wash the wok and it is now ready for use.

CAST IRON GRIDDLE

This thick, flat, heavy plate is made of cast iron. In the Indian kitchen, it is used for cooking chapatti. Place it over the stovetop just as you would any other pan. This versatile griddle can also be used for cooking meats and fish.

COLANDER

This looks like a large metal bowl with many holes and a stand or legs. Colanders come in different sizes and and it is useful to have two or three colanders on hand when preparing a meal. The holes allow water to drain from ingredients placed in them. Some colanders come with a flat base and this prevents the food at the bottom from being crushed.

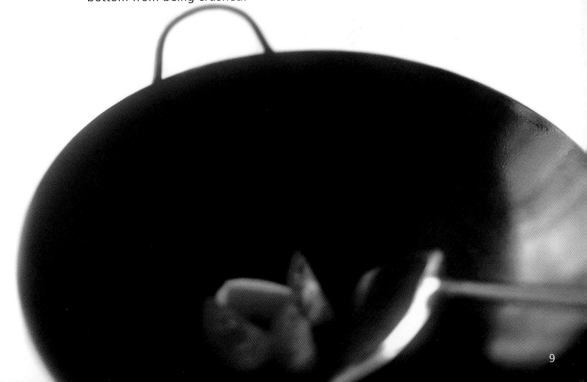

MORTAR AND PESTLE

There are various types of mortar and pestles available. In Indian cooking, the stone or ceramic types are used. They have unglazed surfaces and are slightly abrasive which helps in grinding both wet and dry ingredients. When grinding spices or seeds using a mortar and pestle, the ground ingredients are unevenly broken, a quality which some cooks prefer, as they feel the flavour of the ingredients is enhanced. Unevenly broken ingredients also add texture to the final dish. Having a mortar and pestle on hand is also useful when you need to quickly pound a small amount of chilli, garlic or ginger, or crack open a nutmeg.

ELECTRIC RICE COOKER

Electric rice cookers are readily available with many functions to cook rice, porridge, soups, stews and desserts. Most rice cookers come with instructions to cook various amounts of rice. Wash and place the required amount of rice into the rice cooker, then add the recommended amount of water to cook the rice.

ELECTRIC BLENDER (FOOD PROCESSOR)

This is a most handy gadget to have in the kitchen. Blenders come with many useful attachments that make whipping up a meal a breeze. Blenders are helpful in making sauces, purées and pastes even in small amounts. For Indian cooking, choose one that grinds both dry and wet spices. This will enable you to grind roasted cumin seeds, black and white peppercorns, fennel and roasted dried chillies into fine powders, then mix them into smooth pastes. These spices release their fragrance fully when ground and they are most effective when freshly ground, making the blender an especially useful tool in the Indian kitchen. Some blenders also come with an additional attachment to chop or slice onions.

WOODEN SPOONS

These are sometimes preferred to the metal spoons, as they will not scratch the base of non-stick pots and pans, and they are poor conductors of heat. Wooden spoons generally have long handles for ease when using. Rounded wooden spoons can be used for stirring soups and curries, while wooden spoons with an angled point can be used for sautéing food round in a pan or getting under an ingredient and flipping it over.

WHISKS

The handheld whisk has slightly flexible wires so that it easily incorporates air into batters, creams, sauces, yoghurts and butter when used. Whisks are available in different sizes. Smaller whisks are useful for blending small amounts of sauces or yoghurt, while larger whisks are useful for introducing air into batters and creams. Choose a whisk that fits comfortably into your hand. Ensure that the wires are firmly attached to the handle.

PRESSURE COOKER

The pressure cooker is increasingly popular as a kitchen tool in India. Once the pressure cooker is sealed, pressure builds up inside it and this allows liquid in the pot to rise in temperature. This higher temperature causes food to be cooked faster. Cooking food using a pressure cooker can be three to four times faster than using a pan over the stove. Pressure cookers are usually used when a dish calls for braising or simmering over long periods of time.

WEIGHTS & MEASURES

Quantities for this book are given in Metric, Imperial and American (spoon and cup) measures. Standard spoon and cup measurements used are: 1 tsp = 5 ml, 1 Tbsp = 15 ml, 1 cup = 250 ml. All measures are level unless otherwise stated.

Liquid And Volume Measures

Metric	Imperial	American
5 ml	$1/6$ fl oz	1 teaspoon
10 ml	$1/3$ fl oz	1 dessertspoon
15 ml	$1/2$ fl oz	1 tablespoon
60 ml	2 fl oz	$1/4$ cup (4 tablespoons)
85 ml	$2 1/2$ fl oz	$1/3$ cup
90 ml	3 fl oz	$3/8$ cup (6 tablespoons)
125 ml	4 fl oz	$1/2$ cup
180 ml	6 fl oz	$3/4$ cup
250 ml	8 fl oz	1 cup
300 ml	10 fl oz ($1/2$ pint)	$1 1/4$ cups
375 ml	12 fl oz	$1 1/2$ cups
435 ml	14 fl oz	$1 3/4$ cups
500 ml	16 fl oz	2 cups
625 ml	20 fl oz (1 pint)	$2 1/2$ cups
750 ml	24 fl oz ($1 1/5$ pints)	3 cups
1 litre	32 fl oz ($1 3/5$ pints)	4 cups
1.25 litres	40 fl oz (2 pints)	5 cups
1.5 litres	48 fl oz ($2 2/5$ pints)	6 cups
2.5 litres	80 fl oz (4 pints)	10 cups

Oven Temperature

	°C	°F	Gas Regulo
Very slow	120	250	1
Slow	150	300	2
Moderately slow	160	325	3
Moderate	180	350	4
Moderately hot	190/200	375/400	5/6
Hot	210/220	410/425	6/7
Very hot	230	450	8
Super hot	250/290	475/550	9/10

Dry Measures

Metric	Imperial
30 grams	1 ounce
45 grams	$1 1/2$ ounces
55 grams	2 ounces
70 grams	$2 1/2$ ounces
85 grams	3 ounces
100 grams	$3 1/2$ ounces
110 grams	4 ounces
125 grams	$4 1/2$ ounces
140 grams	5 ounces
280 grams	10 ounces
450 grams	16 ounces (1 pound)
500 grams	1 pound, $1 1/2$ ounces
700 grams	$1 1/2$ pounds
800 grams	$1 3/4$ pounds
1 kilogram	2 pounds, 3 ounces
1.5 kilograms	3 pounds, $4 1/2$ ounces
2 kilograms	4 pounds, 6 ounces

Length

Metric	Imperial
0.5 cm	$1/4$ inch
1 cm	$1/2$ inch
1.5 cm	$3/4$ inch
2.5 cm	1 inch

Abbreviation

tsp	teaspoon
Tbsp	tablespoon
g	gram
kg	kilogram
ml	millilitre

RICE & BREAD

Fried Bread (Bhatura)

Claypot Rice with Spicy Pepper Chicken

Urad Dhal Dumplings with Yoghurt (Dahi Vadai)

Indian-style Fried Rice

Fruit and Nut Pilaf

Savoury Rice Balls (Kozhakatta)

Fried Noodles (Mee Goreng)

Lentils in Puffed Bread (Mung Dhal Puri)

Prawn Pilaf

FRIED BREAD (BHATURA)

This bread goes well with spicy curries. The vegetable shortening gives the bread a light and flaky texture. If you are unable to obtain vegetable shortening, substitute with ghee (clarified butter).

Rub the shortening into the flour using your fingertips. This ensures that the final fried bread is light and flaky in texture.

When kneading the dough, use the ball of your palm.

When ready, the fried bread will bloat up and be golden brown in colour. Remove from oil using a perforated spatula to drain away the oil.

INGREDIENTS

Plain (all-purpose) flour	250 g (9 oz / 2 cups)
Bicarbonate of soda	$1/2$ tsp
Sugar	1 Tbsp
Salt	to taste
Vegetable shortening	1 Tbsp
Plain yoghurt	3 Tbsp
Warm water	250 ml (8 fl oz / 1 cup)
Ghee (clarified butter)	1 Tbsp, melted
Cooking oil for deep-frying	

METHOD

- Sift flour with bicarbonate of soda, sugar and salt. Rub shortening into mixture until it resembles fine breadcrumbs. Warm yoghurt over a low flame. This will sour the yoghurt.

- Pour warmed yoghurt a little at a time into flour mixture while kneading. When yoghurt has been used up, add warm water a little at a time and continue to knead for another 5 minutes.

- Add ghee and knead to a fine, smooth dough. Cover with a dry cloth and set aside for at least 1 hour. Divide dough into 10 lemon-sized balls and dust generously with some flour. Dust rolling board and rolling pin with flour. Roll dough balls into discs.

- Heat oil in a wok. When oil is hot, fry bhaturas one at a time until they bloat up and are golden brown in colour. Drain in a colander lined with absorbent paper.

- Serve hot with a spicy curry.

CLAYPOT RICE WITH SPICY PEPPER CHICKEN

This is an easy one-dish meal, inspired by the popular Chinese claypot recipe. Here, spices are added to excite the taste buds.

Cut the chicken into pieces of similar size. This will ensure that it cooks evenly.

Stir-fry without adding any water. The chicken will cook in its own juices.

Place the cooked ingredients on top of the semi-cooked rice. The rice will absorb the flavour of the stir-fried ingredients.

INGREDIENTS

Chicken	1, about 1 kg (2 lb 3 oz)
Cooking oil	1 1/2 Tbsp
Onion	1, peeled and sliced
Garlic	3 cloves, peeled and minced
Ground white pepper	1 Tbsp
Ground black pepper	1 Tbsp
Salt	1 tsp
Curry leaves	1 stalk
Cumin powder	1 tsp
Chilli powder	1/2 Tbsp
Dark soy sauce	1 Tbsp

GINGER AND GARLIC PASTE

Garlic	5 cloves, peeled and chopped
Ginger	1-cm (1/2-in) knob, peeled and chopped

RICE

Long grain (or Basmati) rice	370 g (13 oz / 2 cups)
Water	750 ml (24 fl oz / 3 cups)
Salt	1/2 tsp
Screwpine (*pandan*) leaves	2, crushed and tied into a knot

GARNISH

Fried shallots	1 1/2 Tbsp
Spring onions (scallions)	55 g (2 oz / 1/2 cup), chopped
Fried cashew nuts	
Fried raisins or sultanas	
Red and green chilli slices	

METHOD

- Cut chicken into 12–14 equal sized pieces. Smaller pieces will cook faster.

- Heat oil in a wok and add onion and garlic. Allow to brown slightly, then add chicken and keep frying until colour changes.

- Add in all remaining ingredients for chicken. (Do not add any water to the wok.) Mix well, then lower heat and prepare rice.

- Blend ingredients for ginger and garlic paste together.

- Wash and drain rice completely. Put rice, water, ginger and garlic paste, salt and screwpine leaves into a clay pot. Bring to the boil and stir. Reduce heat, cover and cook for a further 5 minutes.

- Uncover pot and place chicken over rice. Replace cover and cook for 10–12 minutes over very low heat to prevent burning. Garnish and serve immediately.

URAD DHAL DUMPLINGS WITH YOGHURT (DAHI VADAI)

These dumplings are eaten with cold yoghurt and piquant chutney. This dish is popular in Mumbai's many chaat outlets.

INGREDIENTS

Urad dhal	100 g (3$\frac{1}{2}$ oz / $\frac{1}{2}$ cup)
Rice	$\frac{1}{2}$ Tbsp
Water	125 ml (4 fl oz / $\frac{1}{2}$ cup)
Salt	
Cooking oil for deep-frying	
Thick yoghurt	375 ml (12 fl oz / 1$\frac{1}{2}$ cups)
Sugar	1 Tbsp
Chilli powder	a pinch
Roasted cumin powder	a pinch
Turmeric powder	a pinch

TAMARIND CHUTNEY

Tamarind pulp	100 g (3$\frac{1}{2}$ oz)
Water	300 ml (10 fl oz / 1$\frac{1}{4}$ cups)
Salt	to taste
Dark brown sugar	300 g (11 oz / 1$\frac{1}{3}$ cups)
Chilli powder	1 tsp

GARNISH

Coriander (cilantro) leaves	1 Tbsp minced
Curry leaves	1 stalk, minced
Fine muruku (*sev*)	
Pomegranate seeds	

Use a teaspoon to scoop the batter and another teaspoon to form the batter into small balls. Drop the balls gently into the hot oil.

Soaking the fried dumplings in water will help soften them and remove any excess oil.

Squeeze water out from the dumplings using your hands. The dumplings will gradually spring back to shape.

METHOD

- Soak urad dhal and rice for at least 2 hours and drain well. Pour urad dhal and rice into a blender, then add water and process to a paste.

- Pour paste into a bowl, add a pinch of salt and mix vigorously.

- Heat oil for deep-frying. Drop spoonfuls of batter into oil and fry to a golden brown. Remove and drop into a basin of water. Leave for about 20 minutes, then drain, squeeze and set aside.

- Whisk yoghurt, a pinch of salt and sugar in a large bowl. Place dumplings in to soak for 30 minutes.

- Prepare tamarind chutney. Mix tamarind pulp and water and strain. Combine tamarind water with remaining ingredients. Bring to the boil, then lower heat and simmer until a thick consistency (similar to pancake batter) is achieved. This chutney can be kept indefinitely if stored in the refrigerator.

- Serve dumplings with a good helping of yoghurt. Sprinkle chilli, cumin and turmeric powders and coriander and curry leaves over. Drizzle with tamarind chutney and garnish with muruku and pomegranate seeds.

INDIAN-STYLE FRIED RICE

This is a quick and easy-to-prepare dish. You can add any leftover meats to it for a variation to this recipe.

Cooking the egg before frying the rice helps to grease and season the wok. The rice is less likely to stick to the wok.

Roll up the cooked omelette and slice it into long, thin strips.

Toss the ingredients quickly in the wok to mix and heat through.

INGREDIENTS

Eggs	2, lightly beaten with a dash of pepper
Cooking oil	2 Tbsp
Curry leaves	2 stalks
Onion	1, peeled and sliced
Green chillies	2, sliced
Garlic	5 cloves, peeled and minced
Prawns (shrimps)	200 g (7 oz), peeled and deveined
Carrot	80 g (3 oz / 1 1/2 cups), peeled and grated
Cabbage	100 g (3 1/2 oz / 1 cup), shredded
Chilli paste	1 Tbsp
Salt	to taste
Freshly ground black pepper	1 tsp
Chilli sauce	1 Tbsp
Dark soy sauce	1 Tbsp
Light soy sauce	1 tsp
Cooked rice	400 g (14 1/3 oz / 2 cups)
Green peas	100 g (3 1/2 oz / 2/3 cup)

METHOD

- Prepare eggs for garnish. Heat some oil in a wok and pour in egg to coat wok. When egg is cooked, remove and leave to cool. Roll cooled egg up and slice into strips. Set aside.

- Heat oil in a wok. Add curry leaves, onion, green chillies and garlic and sauté until fragrant.

- Add prawns, carrot and cabbage and stir well. Add chilli paste, salt, pepper, and chilli sauce. Stir in dark and light soy sauces.

- Fluff up cooked rice with a wooden spoon and add to ingredients in wok. Turn up heat to high and very quickly mix ingredients well.

- Sprinkle in peas and heat through. Serve hot with fried egg strips and garnish as desired.

FRUIT AND NUT PILAF

This basic rice dish is a perfect accompaniment to almost every meat, poultry, seafood or vegetable dish in this book.

Stir-fry the spices in the ghee to infuse it with the fragrance of the spices.

Coat the rice well with the spice-infused ghee so it will be fragrant when cooked.

Add colouring to the cooked rice. The grains need not be evenly coated.

Note: The basic rule of cooking rice is to use 1¼ cups water for every 1 cup rice (washed and well-drained).

INGREDIENTS

Ghee (clarified butter)	4 Tbsp
Cinnamon stick	1
Cardamom	5 pods
Cloves	5
Screwpine (*pandan*) leaves	2, tied into a knot
Onions	2, peeled and sliced
Basmati rice	400 g (14¹⁄₃ oz / 2 cups), washed and drained
Water	750 ml (24 fl oz / 3 cups)
Salt	to taste
Saffron strands	10, crushed with the back of a spoon
Yellow food colouring	¹⁄₄ tsp, mixed 1 Tbsp water

GINGER AND GARLIC PASTE

Ginger	1-cm (¹⁄₂-in) knob, peeled and chopped
Garlic	5 cloves, peeled and chopped

GARNISH

Raisins or sultanas	10, fried
Cashew nuts	10, fried
Shallots	5, peeled, sliced and crisp-fried

METHOD

- Blend ingredients for ginger and garlic paste together. Set aside.

- Heat ghee in a wok and add cinnamon, cardamom, cloves and screwpine leaves. Stir to infuse.

- After 2–3 minutes, add onions and stir-fry until golden brown.

- Add rice and stir to coat with spice-infused ghee. Add garlic and ginger paste, and stir well to combine.

- Transfer ingredients to a rice cooker and add water, salt and saffron. Give it a quick stir and switch on rice cooker.

- When rice is cooked, add yellow colouring.

- Use a fork to fluff up rice, then stir in half the garnish and top with remaining half. Serve hot with a spicy curry.

SAVOURY RICE BALLS (KOZHAKATTA)

This is a very old recipe from Kerala. These rice balls can be eaten as a sweet snack or as part of a main meal with curry.

INGREDIENTS

Rice	190 g (6¹/₂ oz / 1 cup), soaked for at least 2 hours and drained
Water	125 ml (4 fl oz / ¹/₂ cup)
Grated coconut	100 g (3¹/₂ oz / 1¹/₄ cup)
Salt	1¹/₂ tsp
Cooking oil	¹/₂ Tbsp
Mustard seeds	1 tsp
Curry leaves	2 stalks

METHOD

- Process soaked rice and water in a blender into a grainy paste.

- Add grated coconut and pulse to blend. Remove from blender and stir in salt.

- Heat oil in a wok. Add mustard seeds and curry leaves. When seeds begin to pop, pour in blended ingredients.

- Add salt and stir until mixture changes to a translucent white and comes away from sides of wok. Turn off heat and allow to cool slightly.

- Meanwhile, get the steamer going.

- Divide rice dough into 24 equal portions. Shape each portion into a ball with your hands. (Oil your hands before handling dough to prevent sticking.)

- Line a tray with a piece of banana leaf and place dough balls on it. Steam for about 10 minutes.

- Serve hot with grated coconut and brown sugar or a good curry.

When blended, the rice and water will become a thick, grainy white paste.

It is important to keep stirring the paste as it cooks to ensure that it is cooked thoroughly.

Oil your hands well before handling the dough to prevent it from sticking to your hands. The balls should be the size of small limes.

FRIED NOODLES (MEE GORENG)

Mee goreng simply means fried noodles. The tomato ketchup gives these noodles an appetising red colour.

INGREDIENTS

Mutton	200 g (7 oz), diced
Ginger and garlic paste	1 tsp (page 18)
Cooking oil	2 Tbsp
Onions	2, peeled and sliced
Garlic	4 cloves, peeled and chopped
Potato	1, peeled and cubed
Bean sprouts	50 g (1²/₃ oz)
Bean curd squares	2, diced
Flowering cabbage (*choy sum*)	5 stalks or any other green vegetable, cut into 5-cm (2¹/₂-in) lengths
Eggs	2, lightly beaten
Tomato ketchup	2 Tbsp
Dark soy sauce	1 Tbsp
Salt	to taste
Yellow egg noodles	300 g (11 oz)
Flat rice noodles	100 g (3¹/₂ oz)
Chinese chives	1–2 stalks, cut into 2¹/₂-cm (1-in) lengths
Limes	

CHILLI PASTE

Dried red chillies	10, soaked in hot water to soften
Garlic	2 cloves, peeled

Fry the chilli paste until it is fragrant and oil begins to separate from the paste.

Add the eggs to the noodles. The eggs will cook in the heat of the noodles.

Break the noodles up using a spatula.

METHOD

- Boil mutton pieces with ginger and garlic paste until tender. Drain and reserve stock for use later.

- Blend ingredients for chilli paste together.

- Heat oil in a wok and stir-fry onions and garlic until fragrant. Add chilli paste and fry until oil separates.

- Now start working really fast. Add mutton, potato cubes, bean sprouts, bean curd and flowering cabbage. Stir quickly.

- Add eggs and allow to set slightly. Add tomato ketchup, soy sauce and salt. Finally, add noodles and mix well over high heat. Keep mixing and breaking noodles up into shorter lengths.

- Taste for seasoning and adjust as necessary.

- Drizzle some reserved stock over noodles if you find it too dry.

- Sprinkle with Chinese chives and serve hot with lime halves.

LENTILS ON PUFFED BREAD
(MUNG DHAL PURI)

Puris are small, puffed breads that are usually eaten for breakfast or dinner with spicy curries.

Roll the balls of dough into discs using a pastry rolling pin.

Smear the discs of dough with the mung bean mixture. Apply a bit of pressure to ensure that the mixture sticks to the dough when fried.

Test if the oil is hot enough before frying the dough. Do this by throwing in a small ball of dough. If the dough floats up almost immediately, the oil is hot enough.

INGREDIENTS

Mutton	200 g (7oz), diced
Split mung beans	100 g (3^1/$_2$ oz / ^{1}/$_2$ cup)
Plain (all-purpose) flour	95 g (3^1/$_2$ oz / ^{3}/$_4$ cup)
Atta (whole wheat) flour	90 g (3 oz / ^{1}/$_2$ cup)
Salt	^{1}/$_2$ tsp
Vegetable shortening	1^1/$_2$ Tbsp
Water	250 ml (8 fl oz / 1 cup)
Onion	1, peeled and finely minced
Green chilli	1, finely minced
Red chilli	1, finely minced
Coriander leaves (cilantro)	1 sprig, finely minced
Cooking oil for deep-frying	

METHOD

- Soak mung beans for at least 2 hours to soften. Drain well before using.

- Sift both types of flour with salt. Rub in shortening and add water slowly. You may not need to use all the water. Knead to a smooth silky dough. Set aside and cover with a dry tea towel.

- Place mung beans, onion, chillies and coriander leaves in a blender and pulse until ingredients bind. (Do not grind until too smooth. Leave a bit of un-ground dhal to give puris a more interesting texture.)

- Divide dough into lime-sized balls. Heat oil for deep-frying.

- Roll balls of dough into discs and smear with mung bean mixture. Pat lightly to help mixture adhere to dough.

- Deep-fry dough to a golden brown and drain well. Serve hot with a spicy curry.

PRAWN PILAF

This is a very fragrant rice dish.

Stir-fry the ingredients for the masala until fragrant. The onions will soften and start to brown.

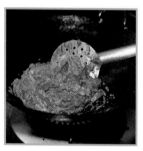

When the tomatoes are soft, add the chilli and tomato paste.

Allow the gravy to cook over medium heat until slightly thick.

INGREDIENTS

Prawns (shrimps)	1 kg (2 lb 3 oz), medium, cleaned
Old ginger	5 slices
Water	1 litre (32 fl oz / 4 cups)
Cooking oil or ghee (clarified butter)	3 Tbsp
Cinnamon sticks	2
Cardamom	4 pods
Cloves	4
Onions	2, peeled and sliced
Ginger	2.5-cm knob (1 in), peeled and minced
Garlic	4 cloves, peeled and minced
Basmati rice	300 g (11 oz / 2 cups), washed and drained
Salt	to taste

PRAWN MASALA

Cooking oil	2 Tbsp
Onions	2, peeled and sliced
Ajwain (celery seeds)	1/4 tsp
Green chillies	3, sliced
Garlic	5 cloves, peeled and minced
Tomatoes	2, finely chopped
Chilli paste	2 Tbsp
Tomato paste	2 tsp
Plain yoghurt	125 ml (4 fl oz / 1/2 cup)
Salt	to taste
Sugar	1 tsp

PASTE

Grated coconut	100 g (3 1/2 oz)
Garlic	4 cloves, peeled
Tomatoes	2, chopped
Coriander leaves (cilantro)	1 sprig, washed and drained

GARNISH

Fried cashew nuts and raisins

METHOD

- Place prawns in a saucepan with slices of ginger. Add water and simmer for 30 minutes. Peel prawns and reserve meat for masala. Set stock aside. Heat oil/ghee in a pan. Add cinnamon, cardamom and cloves. Add onions, ginger and garlic. Fry until onions brown.

- Add rice and fry for 2–3 minutes. Pour in 750 ml (24 fl oz / 3 cups) prawn stock and add salt. Stir and bring to the boil. Reduce heat. Cover and cook until water has evaporated and rice is fluffy. Loosen rice with a wooden spoon. Set aside. Combine paste ingredients and grind.

- Prepare masala. Heat oil in a wok and add ajwain then onions, green chillies and garlic. Stir-fry until fragrant.

- Add tomatoes and when softened, add chilli and tomato pastes. Stir-fry for 2 minutes then add ground paste. Cook for at least 5 minutes over medium heat.

- Add prawns, yoghurt, salt and sugar and cook until gravy is slightly thick. To serve, line a bowl with pilaf rice then add some prawn masala. Continue to layer to fill bowl. Garnish with fried cashew nuts and raisins to serve. Add a few unpeeled prawns as garnish as desired.

VEGETABLES & EGG

Chilli Bean Curd

Egg Curry (*Moota Kari*)

Aubergines in Yoghurt (*Eggplant Raita*)

Green Bananas in Yoghurt (*Plantain Kaalan*)

Ginger Chutney (*Inji Puli*)

Mixed Vegetables with Dhal (*Kootu Kari*)

Malayalee Stir-fry (*Mezhakeperatti*)

Mock Duck Special

Cottage Cheese Bhurjee (*Paneer Bhurjee*)

Pumpkin Chutney

Curried Ridge Gourd (*Ridge Gourd Theeyal*)

CHILLI BEAN CURD

Use firm bean curd squares for this recipe. This dish is perfect for those days when you wish to go vegetarian.

To prepare tamarind juice, knead the tamarind pulp in the water to separate the pulp and seeds.

When the tamarind pulp has been loosened from the seeds, strain the juice through a sieve.

Ensure that the bean curd is dry before adding to the hot oil to fry, or the oil will splatter.

INGREDIENTS

Tamarind pulp	30 g (1 oz)
Water	60 ml (2 fl oz / $^1/_4$ cup)
Cooking oil for deep-frying	
Firm bean curd	6 squares
Onions	2, peeled and sliced
Garlic	4 cloves, peeled and sliced
Chilli sauce	$1^1/_2$ Tbsp
Salt	to taste
Sugar	1 Tbsp
Tomatoes	3, cut into quarters
Spring onion (scallion)	1, cut into 2.5-cm (1-in) lengths

CHILLI PASTE

Dried red chillies	15
Garlic	5 cloves, peeled
Shallots	6, peeled
Water	125 ml (4 fl oz / $^1/_2$ cup)

METHOD

- Combine tamarind pulp and water and knead to separate pulp from seeds. Strain liquid and set aside.

- Blend ingredients for chilli paste in a blender. Set aside.

- Cut bean curd into large cubes and pat-dry. Heat oil and deep-fry bean curd until golden brown. Drain and set aside.

- Leaving about $2^1/_2$ Tbsp in the pan, reheat and stir-fry chilli paste until fragrant and oil floats to the surface. Add sliced onions and garlic.

- Pour in tamarind juice and simmer for about 10 minutes.

- Add fried bean curd cubes, chilli sauce, salt and sugar, and cook until bean curd has absorbed the flavours.

- Add tomatoes and spring onion. Serve hot.

EGG CURRY (MOOTA KARI)

This egg curry is a good alternative to the usual vegetable or meat curries.

When boiling eggs, add them to room temperature water, then bring to the boil. This way, the eggs will not crack.

Stir-fry the onions until they turn golden brown in colour and are fragrant.

Check that the potatoes are soft by pressing one with a wooden spoon or spatula. It should yield to the pressure of the wooden spoon or spatula.

INGREDIENTS

Garlic	6 cloves, peeled and chopped
Ginger	2.5-cm (1-in) knob, peeled and chopped
Cooking oil	60 ml (2 fl oz / $^1/_4$ cup)
Cinnamon	1 stick
Cardamom	5 pods
Star anise	1
Curry leaves	3 stalks
Onions	2, peeled and sliced
Potatoes	3, peeled and quartered
Tomatoes	4, quartered
Water	500 ml (16 fl oz / 2 cups)
Eggs	10, hard-boiled and peeled
Evaporated milk	125 ml (4 fl oz / $^1/_2$ cup)
Mustard seeds	2 tsp
Shallots	4, peeled and sliced

CURRY PASTE

Meat curry powder	2 Tbsp
Chilli powder	$^1/_2$ Tbsp
Ground black pepper	$^1/_2$ tsp or use ground white pepper if you prefer the dish to be spicer
Water	60 ml (2 fl oz / $^1/_4$ cup)
Salt	to taste

METHOD

- Blend garlic and ginger into a paste and set aside. Combine curry paste ingredients and set aside.

- Heat oil in a pan and stir-fry cinnamon, cardamom, star anise and a stalk of curry leaves.

- Add onions and stir-fry to a golden brown. Add garlic-ginger paste and simmer until fragrant before adding curry paste. Cook for 3–5 minutes.

- Add potatoes, half the tomatoes and water and cook until potatoes are almost done. Add hard-boiled eggs and evaporated milk. Simmer for 15 minutes, then add remaining tomatoes.

- Meanwhile, heat some oil in a wok. Fry mustard seeds, remaining curry leaves and shallots. When shallots brown, pour over simmering curry.

- Allow curry to stand for 30 minutes before serving.

AUBERGINE IN YOGHURT
(EGGPLANT RAITA)

This dish is perfect as a dip with crackers or as a side dish.

INGREDIENTS

Cooking oil for deep-frying	
Long purple aubergines (brinjals/eggplants)	3
Plain yoghurt	250 ml (8 fl oz / 1 cup)
Green chillies	3
Cumin seeds	$^1/_2$ tsp
Grated coconut	5 Tbsp
White peppercorns	1 tsp
Salt	to taste
Curry leaves	2 stalks

METHOD

- Heat oil for deep-frying.

- Cut aubergines into thin discs and fry immediately. Fry discs until golden brown, then drain well and set aside.

- Process remaining ingredients in a blender except for 1 stalk of curry leaves.

- Pour mixture into a wok and add remaining stalk of curry leaves. Allow mixture to come to the boil slowly.

- Add aubergines and serve immediately.

Slice aubergines into thin discs and use immediately. Cut aubergines will oxidise and turn dark if left uncooked for too long.

Slide the aubergine discs gently into the hot oil.

Remove the fried discs from the hot oil using a slotted spoon to drain the oil.

GREEN BANANAS IN YOGHURT SAUCE (PLANTAIN KAALAN)

Green bananas or plantains are very versatile. The green ones can be used in curries and the ripe ones in desserts. If you are unable to find green bananas, omit or substitute with pumpkin.

Cut the winter melon into quarters, then slice away the seeds.

As green bananas are unripe, the skin does not peel readily. Use a knife.

Use a small frying pan to temper the ingredients.

INGREDIENTS

Green bananas (plantains)	2
Pumpkin	200 g (7 oz), peeled and cut into chunks
Winter melon	1, about 300 g (11 oz)
Yam	1 (optional)
Green chillies	3
Water	500 ml (16 fl oz / 2 cups)
Turmeric powder	1 tsp
Chilli powder	1/2 tsp (optional)
Ground black or white pepper	2 tsp
Salt	1 tsp

TURMERIC SOLUTION

Water	250 ml (8 fl oz / 1 cup)
Turmeric powder	1/2 tsp

PASTE

Thick yoghurt	250 ml (8 fl oz / 1 cup)
Grated coconut	100 g (3 1/2 oz / 1 1/4 cups)
Cumin seeds	1 tsp
Curry leaves	1 stalk

TEMPERING

Cooking oil	2 Tbsp
Mustard seeds	1 tsp
Fenugreek seeds	1/2 tsp
Curry leaves	2 stalks
Dried red chillies	2, each cut into 3

METHOD

- Prepare turmeric solution by mixing water and turmeric powder. Set aside. Rub hands and a knife with some cooking oil. (This makes it easier to wash away the sap from the green bananas.) Peel and cut green bananas into chunks. Place into turmeric solution for 5 minutes to prevent oxidization.

- Peel and cut winter melon, pumpkin and yam, if using, into chunks. Place into the same turmeric solution for 5 minutes.

- Drain bananas, winter melon, pumpkin and yam and wash. Place chunks of vegetables and green chillies into a saucepan with water. Add turmeric and chilli powders, pepper and salt. Bring to the boil, then reduce to medium heat. Allow vegetables to cook until tender but not mushy.

- Meanwhile, combine paste ingredients and grind into a paste. (Do not add any water). Add paste to cooking vegetables. Keep stirring to prevent curdling. When well combined, leave to simmer for another 10 minutes.

- To temper, heat oil and add tempering ingredients. When chillies brown, pour mixture over vegetables. Stir and set aside for 30 minutes before serving.

GINGER CHUTNEY (INJI PULI)

With careful handling, this chutney will keep in the refrigerator for up to a year.

INGREDIENTS

Tamarind pulp	100 g (3^1/$_2$ oz)
Water	250 ml (8 fl oz / 1 cup)
Cooking oil	60 ml (2 fl oz / ^{1}/$_4$ cup)
Mustard seeds	1 tsp
Fenugreek seeds	^{1}/$_2$ tsp
Curry leaves	2 stalks
Ginger	500 g (1 lb 1^1/$_2$ oz / 3 cups), peeled and minced
Green chillies	6, minced
Salt	to taste
Chilli powder	^{1}/$_2$ Tbsp
Brown sugar	180 g (6^1/$_2$ oz / ^{3}/$_4$ cup)

METHOD

- Knead tamarind pulp in water. Strain liquid and set aside.

- Heat oil in a wok. When hot, add mustard seeds, fenugreek and curry leaves. When mustard seeds start to splutter, add ginger and green chillies. Fry until fragrant.

- Add salt and chilli powder. Stir well and pour in tamarind water and brown sugar. Leave to simmer until sauce thickens.

- Adjust seasoning to taste, then leave to cool completely before serving. Chutney should be hot and sweet.

Stir-fry the ingredients to mix well.

Add the chilli powder according to taste. Use less if a less spicy chutney is preferred.

Simmer the chutney until it is thick. You should be able to see the minced ginger and chillies on the surface.

MIXED VEGETABLES WITH DHAL
(KOOTU KARI)

This mild curry goes well with spicy dishes such as mutton pepper fry, chicken perattal or fried fish.

Cut the pumpkin into wedges, then peel the skin using a small knife.

Peel the snake gourd using a vegetable peeler.

Slice the snake gourd into half lengthwise. Remove seeds and discard, then cut into small pieces.

INGREDIENTS

Channa dhal (horse gram)	180 g (6¹/₂ oz / 1 cup)
Water	700 ml (24 fl oz / 3 cups)
Potatoes	2, peeled and diced
Pumpkin	100 g (3¹/₂ oz), peeled and diced
Winter melon	100 g (3¹/₂ oz), cut into dices
Carrot	1, peeled and diced
Yam	1, small, peeled and diced
Snake gourd	1, peeled and diced
Green chillies	3, chopped
Onion	1, peeled and chopped
Turmeric powder	1 tsp
Chilli powder	¹/₂ Tbsp
Salt	to taste
Coconut milk	125 ml (4 fl oz / ¹/₂ cup)

PASTE

Grated coconut	50 g (1²/₃ oz / ¹/₂ cup, packed)
Cumin seeds	1 tsp
Garlic	2 cloves, peeled
Water	125 ml (4 fl oz / ¹/₂ cup)

TEMPERING

Cooking oil	1¹/₂ Tbsp
Mustard seeds	1 tsp
Uncooked rice	1 tsp
Dried red chillies	2, each cut into 3 sections
Curry leaves	2 stalks

METHOD

- Combine ingredients for paste in a blender and process. Set aside.

- Boil dhal in water until soft. Add vegetables, turmeric and chilli powders and salt. Mix well.

- Add half the coconut milk and cook until vegetables are almost done.

- Add paste and stir. Simmer for about 10 minutes before adding remaining coconut milk.

- Heat oil for tempering and add mustard seeds, rice, chillies and curry leaves. Heat until mustard seeds start to splutter. Pour into curry.

- Serve hot with white rice or bread and crispy pappadums.

MALAYALEE STIR-FRY (MEZHAKEPERATTI)

This is a colourful vegetarian dish. It uses both dried red chillies and green chillies, so it can be rather spicy even though it looks mild.

Cut the vegetables into similar-sized pieces so they will cook more evenly. Drain the vegetables when you are ready to cook them.

Leave the ingredients to cook until all the water has evaporated.

Check that the vegetables are tender using a fork. The fork should cut through the vegetables effortlessly.

INGREDIENTS

Green bananas	2, peeled and diced
Sweet potato	1, peeled and diced
Long beans	10, cut into 2.5-cm (1-in) lengths
Cooking oil	2 Tbsp
Mustard seeds	1 tsp
Curry leaves	1 stalk
Dried red chillies	2, chopped
Onion	1, peeled and chopped
Green chillies	2, sliced
Salt	to taste

TURMERIC SOLUTION

Turmeric powder	1 tsp
Water	125ml (4 fl oz / $^1/_2$ cup)

METHOD

- Prepare turmeric solution by mixing water and turmeric powder. Put long beans, bananas and sweet potato in to soak to prevent oxidization.

- Rub hands and a knife with some cooking oil. (This makes it easier to wash away the sap from the green bananas.) Peel and dice green bananas. Place into turmeric solution to prevent oxidization.

- Peel and dice sweet potato. Cut long beans into 1-cm ($^1/_2$-in) lengths. Soak in the same turmeric solution.

- Heat oil in a wok and add mustard seeds, curry leaves and dried red chillies. Allow mustard seeds to splutter before adding onion and green chillies.

- Drain bananas, sweet potato and long beans. Rinse and add to wok. Season to taste with salt, then toss and cover. Leave to cook until water has completely evaporated.

- Cook over low heat for another 10 minutes until vegetables are tender. Serve hot.

MOCK DUCK SPECIAL

Mock duck is prepared from soy and gluten. This is a delightful dish to eat even if you're not vegetarian.

INGREDIENTS

Cooking oil	60 ml (2 fl oz / ¼ cup)
Onions	2, peeled and sliced
Red chillies	2, sliced
Tomatoes	3, sliced
Chilli powder	1 Tbsp
Tomato paste	2 Tbsp
Canned mock duck	3 cans, each 285 g (10 oz), sliced, brine reserved
Salt	to taste
Coriander leaves (cilantro)	1 sprig

METHOD

- Heat oil and stir-fry onions, chillies and tomatoes until soft. Add chilli powder and tomato paste. Mix well.

- Pour in brine from cans and simmer for 15–20 minutes. Adjust to taste with salt.

- Add mock duck slices and mix well. Cook until sauce sizzles at the side of wok.

- Add coriander leaves and serve hot with rice.

Slice the mock duck into thin slices so they will absorb the flavour of the gravy more readily.

Simmer the brine until it becomes a thick gravy.

Cook until the gravy sizzles at the sides of the wok, then add coriander.

COTTAGE CHEESE BHURJEE
(PANEER BHURJEE)

You can eat this dish with rice or Indian breads or use it as a sauce with spaghetti or lasagne.

To mince garlic, slice the peeled garlic, then cut the slices into small bits.

Crumble the cottage cheese using your hands. It should break up easily.

Pour the cream into the cottage cheese mixture and mix well.

INGREDIENTS

Cooking oil	125 ml (4 fl oz / ^{1}/$_2$ cup)
Onions	2, peeled and minced
Tomatoes	2, minced
Green chillies	3, minced
Red chillies	2, minced
Garlic	4 cloves, peeled and minced
Cottage cheese (paneer)	1 kg (2 lb 3 oz), crumbled
Chilli powder	3 tsp
Roasted cumin powder	1 tsp
Masala powder	1 tsp
Salt	to taste
Water	125 ml (4 fl oz / ^{1}/$_2$ cup)
Tomato paste	125 ml (4 fl oz / ^{1}/$_2$ cup)
Cream	125 ml (4 fl oz / ^{1}/$_2$ cup)
Coriander leaves (cilantro)	1 sprig, minced
Sugar	1 tsp
Diced red and yellow capsicums (bell peppers)	

METHOD

- Heat oil in a wok. Add onions, tomatoes, green and red chillies and garlic. Cook until onions begin to brown.

- Add cottage cheese and stir. Add chilli and cumin powders and masala. Add salt and mix well, then pour in water and add tomato paste. Mix well.

- Cover and allow cottage cheese to cook in the sauce and absorb all the flavours.

- Slowly pour in cream and add coriander and sugar. Stir and taste to adjust seasoning.

- Allow flavours to infuse for at least 15 minutes before serving. Garnish with diced capsicums and serve.

PUMPKIN CHUTNEY

Chutneys add flavour and dimension to plain and simple meals. This chutney can also be used as a dip.

INGREDIENTS

Pumpkin	800 g (1 ¾ lb)
Cooking oil	1 ½ Tbsp
Mustard seeds	2 tsp
Curry leaves	2 stalks
Garlic	3 cloves, peeled and minced
Water	60 ml (2 fl oz / ¼ cup)
Chilli powder	1 tsp
Roasted cumin powder	1 tsp
Turmeric powder	1 tsp
Salt	to taste
Brown sugar	1 ½ Tbsp
Ghee (clarified butter)	½ tsp

METHOD

- Cut pumpkin in half and remove pith and seeds. Cut into large chunks and steam until tender.

- Heat oil in a wok and add mustard seeds, curry leaves and garlic. Sauté quickly, then add pumpkin. Stir to mix well.

- Add water, chilli, cumin and turmeric powders and salt. Keep stirring to mix.

- Add brown sugar and keep stirring until flavours are well mixed.

- Add ghee and adjust seasoning to taste. Serve hot with Indian breads.

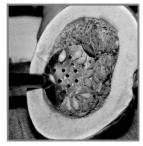
Cut the pumpkin in half, then remove the pith and seeds using a large metal spoon.

Steam the pumpkin until tender. It should break easily when bent.

Stir-fry the chutney to mix the ingredients. You can break the pumpkin into smaller pieces.

CURRIED RIDGE GOURD
(RIDGE GOURD THEEYAL)

In Kerala, every household has their own version of theeyal. This is because any vegetable can be used as long as the thick gravy is left as it is. This dish has a deep flavour and goes well with dosai, rice, breads and idli. I chose to use ridge gourd because of its interesting gritty, crunchy texture.

Roast the dried red chillies using a dry pan. They will trun a darker shade of red.

Wash the ridge gourds thoroughly. Cut into 5-cm sections, then slice thinly.

Roast the grated coconut in a dry pan. Stir continuously to prevent it from burning.

INGREDIENTS

Dried red chillies	6
Coriander	1 tsp
Fenugreek seeds	1/4 tsp
Cumin seeds	1/4 tsp
Grated coconut	90 g (3 oz / 1 cup)
Ridge gourds	2
Cooking oil	1 1/2 Tbsp
Onion	1, peeled and sliced
Red chillies	2, sliced
Green chillies	2, sliced
Curry leaves	2 stalks
Salt	1 1/2 tsp
Turmeric powder	1/4 tsp
Chilli powder	1/4 tsp
Water	435 ml (14 fl oz / 1 3/4 cups)

TAMARIND JUICE

Tamarind pulp	50 g (1 2/3 oz)
Water	125 ml (4 fl oz / 1/2 cup)

TEMPERING

Cooking oil	1 1/2 Tbsp
Mustard seeds	1 tsp
Dried red chillies	2
Curry leaves	1 stalk
Onion	1, peeled and sliced

METHOD

- In a dry pan, roast chillies. Make sure the chillies do not burn or they will taste bitter. Remove chillies then roast coriander, fenugreek and cumin until smoky.

- In the same pan, dry-roast grated coconut to a light brown colour. Combine then grind all roasted ingredients into a paste with 180 ml (6 fl oz / ³/₄ cup) water.

- Wash ridge gourds well. Without peeling skin, slice thinly. Heat oil in a wok and stir-fry ridge gourds quickly. Set aside.

- Prepare tamarind juice. Mix tamarind pulp and water together and strain.

- In a saucepan, place ridge gourd, ground paste, onion, red and green chillies, tamarind juice, curry leaves, salt, turmeric and chilli powders and remaining water. Cook over low heat until ridge gourd is cooked and gravy is fragrant.

- Heat oil for tempering in a wok. Add mustard seeds. When mustard seeds splutter, add chillies, curry leaves and onion. When onion browns, pour mixture over ridge gourd theeyal.

- Leave to simmer for another 5 minutes. Serve hot with rice or breads.

SEAFOOD

Prawns in Spicy Masala (*Chemeen Chammandhi*)

Fenugreek Fried Fish (*Methi Meen Poriyal*)

Fried Fish in Chilli Vinegar

Kerala Fish Curry (*Kerala Meen Kari*)

Fenugreek Fish Curry (*Methi Meen Kari*)

Seafood and Bean Curd Hot Plate

PRAWNS IN SPICY MASALA
(CHEMEEN CHAMMANDHI)

This is a typical South Indian dish with prawns. It is hot and spicy and goes well with rice and a simple stir-fried vegetable dish.

Roast the dried red chillies in a dry wok. Move them around the wok often to prevent them from burning.

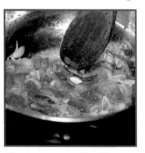

The tomatoes will soften gradually and lose their shape. Once they are soft, add the ground paste.

When the prawns are cooked, they will take on an opaque colour and curl up.

INGREDIENTS

Cooking oil	60 ml (2 fl oz / $^1/_4$ cup)
Onion	1, peeled and sliced
Green chillies	3
Tomatoes	2, chopped
Tiger prawns (shrimps)	1 kg (2 lb 3 oz) , peeled and deveined
Green mango	1, peeled, pitted and sliced
Tamarind pulp	50 g (1$^2/_3$ oz)
Water	125 ml (4 fl oz / $^1/_2$ cup)
Salt	to taste
Curry leaves	2 stalks

PASTE

Dried red chillies	10
Grated coconut	55 g (2 oz / $^1/_2$ cup)
Roasted cumin powder	$^1/_2$ tsp
Black peppercorns	1 tsp
Curry leaves	2 stalks
Shallots	5, peeled
Tamarind pulp	1 tsp
Garlic	2 cloves, peeled
Tomato	1, chopped
Fenugreek seeds	$^1/_2$ tsp

METHOD

- Prepare paste. In a wok, dry-roast dried chillies until smoky. Remove and grind to a paste with all other paste ingredients. Add some water if necessary to get a smooth paste.

- Heat oil in a wok. Sauté onion, green chillies and tomatoes until soft. Add ground paste and keep cooking until fragrant.

- Add prawns and green mango and sauté for 10 minutes.

- Knead tamarind pulp in water and strain. Add tamarind juice, salt and curry leaves to wok. Cook until prawns are done.

- Serve hot with rice or Indian breads.

FENUGREEK FRIED FISH
(METHI MEEN PORIYAL)

Fenugreek and fish go very well together. This recipe uses fenugreek powder that leaves an irresistible aroma in your kitchen.

Combine the fish curry, chilli, fenugreek, turmeric and cumin powders, curry leaves and paste together in a bowl. Ensure that the ingredients are well mixed.

Coat the fish well with a layer of the paste mixture.

Use a spatula to lower the fish gently into the hot oil to avoid the oil splashing up.

INGREDIENTS

Fish (Spanish mackerel or threadfin bream)	4 thick slices, each about 100 g (3¹/₂ oz)
Limes	2, squeezed for juice
Salt	to taste
Fish curry powder	¹/₂ Tbsp
Chilli powder	¹/₂ Tbsp
Fenugreek powder (*methi*)	¹/₂ tsp
Turmeric powder	¹/₂ tsp
Roasted cumin powder	¹/₂ tsp
Chopped curry leaves	1 tsp
Cooking oil for deep-frying	

PASTE

Shallots	10, peeled
Garlic	10 cloves, peeled
Ginger	2.5-cm (1-in) knob

METHOD

- Rub fish with lime juice and salt. Set aside to marinate. Grind shallots, garlic and ginger into a paste.

- Mix fish curry powder, chilli, fenugreek, turmeric and cumin powders, curry leaves and paste together then rub all over fish. Set aside for 30 minutes.

- Heat oil and deep-fry fish to a golden brown.

- Drain fish and serve hot with a fresh garden salad of your choice.

FRIED FISH IN CHILLI VINEGAR

A few slivers of torch ginger bud add a completely new dimension to dishes, especially salads. Torch ginger buds can also be used in floral decorations.

INGREDIENTS

Meaty fish	1 kg (2 lb 3 oz), cut into thick slices
Salt	to taste
Turmeric powder	1 tsp
Cooking oil for deep-frying	
Onions	2, peeled and sliced
Garlic	5 cloves, peeled and minced
Red chillies	2, sliced
Tomatoes	4, quartered
Tamarind pulp	50 g (1²/₃ oz)
Water	125 ml (4 fl oz / ¹/₂ cup)
Chilli sauce	2 Tbsp
Sugar	2 tsp or to taste
Vinegar	3 Tbsp
Coriander (cilantro) leaves	1 sprig, chopped
Torch ginger bud	1, sliced

CHILLI PASTE

Dried red chillies	20, soaked to soften then drained
Garlic	6 cloves, peeled
Shallots	5, peeled
Candlenuts	5

Rub the salt and turmeric powder in the fish. Wear gloves if necessary, since turmeric tends to stain.

Cook the chilli paste in a well ventilated area, as the fumes may irritate your eyes.

Lower the fried fish gently into the gravy using a spatula to avoid breaking it.

METHOD

- Season fish with a dash of salt and turmeric. Set aside for about 20 minutes.

- Combine chilli paste ingredients and grind into a paste. Set aside.

- Heat oil in a wok and deep-fry fish until golden brown. Drain and set aside.

- Leaving about 5 Tbsp oil in the wok, reheat and add onions, garlic, chillies and tomatoes. Sauté until soft.

- Add chilli paste and fry until fragrant.

- Add tamarind juice, chilli sauce, salt and sugar. Bring to the boil then simmer for about 10 minutes until gravy thickens slightly.

- Add fried fish and stir well to let gravy coat fish completely.

- Add vinegar and stir. Adjust seasoning to taste.

- Finish off with coriander leaves and torch ginger bud. Serve hot with rice or bread. Garnish as desired.

KERALA FISH CURRY (KERALA MEEN KARI)

This recipe works best when the fish is very fresh. You can also use a large meaty fish head if preferred. If you don't have a claypot, use an enamel pot.

INGREDIENTS

Meaty fish	600 g (1 lb 5$^1/_3$ oz), cut into chunks
Ground black pepper	1 tsp
Salt	$^1/_2$ Tbsp
Chilli powder	1 Tbsp
Turmeric powder	$^1/_2$ tsp
Cumin powder	1 tsp, roasted
Ginger	2.5-cm (1-in) knob, peeled and minced
Curry leaves	2 sprigs
Green mangoes	3, peeled and sliced, pits reserved
Curry leaves	5 stalks
Tamarind pulp	50 g (1$^2/_3$ oz)
Water	250 ml (8 fl oz / 1 cup)
Cooking oil	1 Tbsp
Fenugreek seeds (*methi*)	$^1/_2$ tsp, roasted, then finely ground

PASTE A

Dried red chillies	15
Shallots	6, peeled

PASTE B

Grated coconut	55 g (2 oz / $^1/_2$ cup)
Cumin seeds	1 tsp
Garlic	6 cloves, peeled

Peel the ginger using a small knife or vegetable peeler.

Peel the green mangoes, then cut them into slices.

The layer of curry leaves at the base of the claypot will help prevent the mango and fish from burning. The flavour of the leaves will also rise up to infuse the fish.

METHOD

- Place fish in a bowl and add pepper, salt, chilli, turmeric and cumin powders and ginger. Rub seasoning into fish.

- Scatter 2 stalks of curry leaves into the base of a seasoned claypot. Layer with sliced mangoes and pits and top with fish. Set aside.

- Combine tamarind pulp and water and strain. Grind paste A ingredients together and mix with tamarind juice. Grind paste B ingredients together and set aside.

- Pour paste A over fish and simmer on low heat. When mixture comes to the boil, add paste B.
  Give claypot a gentle shake and cook for 15 minutes more over low heat. (Do not stir with a ladle
  or spoon or the fish will break up. Use kitchen mittens or a tea towel when handling hot pots.)

- Drizzle oil into curry, then sprinkle fenugreek powder over. Add remaining curry leaves and shake pot again to mix. Adjust seasoning to taste.

- Let curry stand for at least 30 minutes before serving.

FENUGREEK FISH CURRY
(METHI MEEN KARI)

Dried fenugreek (methi) leaves are available at Indian grocers. It is a pungent herb so use sparingly if this is the first time you're using it.

Soften the dried fenugreek leaves in boiling water before using.

Lower the fried fish into the curry sauce gently to avoid splattering the sauce.

Add the cream and yoghurt to the curry sauce and stir gently and carefully to avoid breaking up the pieces of fried fish.

INGREDIENTS

Fish (red snapper/ Spanish mackerel)	500 g (1 lb 1^1/$_2$ oz), cut into thick slices
Chilli powder	^{1}/$_2$ tsp
Salt	1 tsp
Turmeric powder	^{1}/$_4$ tsp
Cooking oil for deep-frying	
Onions	2, peeled and sliced
Green chillies	2, sliced
Red chillies	2, sliced
Tomatoes	3, chopped
Fish curry powder	1^1/$_2$ Tbsp
Chilli powder	2 tsp
Cumin seeds	^{1}/$_2$ tsp, roasted and finely ground
Salt	to taste
Tamarind juice	125 ml (4 fl oz / ^{1}/$_2$ cup)
Water	625 ml (1 pint / 2^1/$_2$ cups)
Dried fenugreek (*methi*) leaves	1^1/$_2$ Tbsp
Coriander leaves (cilantro)	3 sprigs, chopped
Cream	60 ml (2 fl oz / ^{1}/$_4$ cup)
Plain yoghurt	1^1/$_2$ Tbsp

PASTE

Shallots	10, peeled
Garlic	10 cloves, peeled
Ginger	2.5-cm (1-in) knob
Tomatoes	2
Onions	2, peeled, sliced and fried until golden brown

METHOD

- Combine paste ingredients and grind into a paste. Set aside.

- Marinade fish with chilli powder, salt and turmeric. Set aside for 10 minutes.

- Heat oil for deep-frying. Fry fish until golden brown. Drain and set aside.

- Leave 2 Tbsp oil and reheat. Add sliced onions, chillies and tomatoes. Sauté until soft.

- Add ground paste and cook for 5 minutes before adding fish curry, chilli and cumin powders. Add salt and tamarind juice. Bring to a slow boil and simmer to allow flavours to infuse. (This will take 10–15 minutes.)

- In a small pot, bring 250 ml (8 fl oz / 1 cup) water to the boil. Add fenugreek leaves to soften. Strain and discard water. Add leaves to simmering sauce.

- Add fried fish and half the coriander leaves. Cook over low heat for another 10 minutes.

- Add cream and yoghurt, stirring carefully. Taste and adjust seasoning. Add remaining coriander leaves.

- Allow curry to stand for 30 minutes before serving with hot chapatti or rice.

SEAFOOD AND BEAN CURD HOTPLATE

The spiciness of this dish will depend on the number of dried red chillies used. Reduce the number of chillies used if preferred.

Pull the squid's head from its body. The internal organs and quill will follow. Be careful not to break the ink sac. Discard.

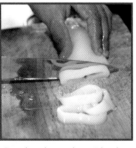

Cut the cleaned squid tube into rings.

To shred the kaffir lime leaves, roll it up then slice finely.

INGREDIENTS

Cooking oil	60 ml (2 fl oz / $^1/_4$ cup)
Egg bean curd	2 tubes, cut into slices
Onion	1, peeled and sliced
Garlic	6 cloves, peeled and minced
Prawns (shrimps)	500 g (1 lb 1$^1/_2$ oz), peeled and deveined
Squid	500 g (1 lb 1$^1/_2$ oz), cleaned and sliced
Oyster sauce	$^1/_2$ Tbsp
Tomato sauce	1 Tbsp
Stock	60 ml (2 fl oz / $^1/_4$ cup)
Chinese chives	1 sprig, chopped or leek (optional)
Spring onion (scallion)	1, chopped
Lime	1, squeezed for juice
Kaffir lime leaves	2, finely shredded
Sugar	to taste
Salt	to taste

CHILLI PASTE

Dried red chillies	8
Shallots	4, peeled
Garlic	4 cloves, peeled
Lemon grass	1 stalk

METHOD

- Combine ingredients for chilli paste and grind into a paste. Set aside.

- Heat enough oil for deep-frying and deep-fry bean curd slices. Drain and set aside. Heat oil in a wok and stir-fry onion and garlic until fragrant.

- Add chilli paste and fry until fragrant. Add prawns and squid and stir well to mix. Add oyster sauce, tomato sauce and stock. Cover and allow seafood to cook for 10 minutes. Add salt and sugar to taste.

- To serve, prepare a hot plate and add a little oil. Arrange fried bean curd slices on hot plate and spoon prawns and squid mixture around and over bean curd. Allow to sizzle for a while, then add chives or leek if using and spring onions. Drizzle lime juice over and top with shredded lime leaves. Serve hot.

- If you do not have a hotplate, do the last step in the wok, then serve immediately.

POULTRY

Butter Chicken

Spicy Chicken Masala (*Chicken Perattal*)

Chicken Tikka

Chicken with Chilli and Capsicums

Easy Chicken Tajine

Tandoori Chicken

BUTTER CHICKEN

The evaporated milk used in this recipe gives it a really enjoyable creaminess.

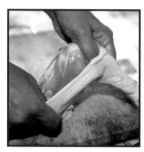

Skin the chicken by pulling the skin away with your hands.

Cut the chicken into smaller pieces with a sharp knife. Cutting along the joints is easier.

Heat the oil and the butter together in a wok. Although using butter alone will make the dish very fragrant, the oil is used to help raise the smoking point of the butter.

INGREDIENTS

Chicken thighs	10, washed, skinned and cut into serving-size portions
Cooking oil	2^1/$_2$ Tbsp
Butter	1 Tbsp
Onions	3, peeled and finely sliced
Curry leaves	2 stalks
Tomatoes	3, chopped
Chilli powder	1 Tbsp
Salt	to taste
Evaporated milk	60 ml (2 fl oz / ^{1}/$_4$ cup)
Cream	1 Tbsp
Coriander leaves (cilantro)	2 sprigs, chopped

MARINADE

Red chillies	3
Onion	^{1}/$_2$, peeled and chopped
Garlic	5 cloves
Ginger	2.5-cm knob (1-in), peeled and chopped
Lime	1, juice extracted
Turmeric powder	^{1}/$_2$ tsp
Sugar	^{1}/$_2$ tsp
Kitchen King masala powder	1 tsp

METHOD

- Blend marinade ingredients into a paste and rub into chicken. Leave to marinate for at least 30 minutes.

- Heat oil and butter in a wok until hot. (The oil raises the smoking point of the butter and prevents it from burning.)

- Add onions, curry leaves and tomatoes and fry until tomatoes are pulpy.

- Add marinated chicken, chilli powder and salt. Cook over a medium-low flame for 30 minutes, stirring occasionally.

- Pour in evaporated milk and add coriander leaves. Mix well, and allow gravy to thicken. Remove from heat.

- Drizzle with cream and garnish with coriander leaves. Serve hot with rice or chapattis.

SPICY CHICKEN MASALA
(CHICKEN PERATTAL)

This is a Kerala-style dish.

INGREDIENTS

Cooking oil	125ml (4 fl oz / $^1/_2$ cup)
Curry leaves	3 stalks
Onions	2, peeled and sliced
Chicken	1, about 1.5 kg (3 lb 4$^1/_2$ oz), cut into serving-size pieces, washed and drained
Salt	to taste
Turmeric powder	$^1/_4$ tsp
Potatoes	3–4, peeled and quartered (optional)
Fennel seeds	2 tsp

PASTE

Cooking oil	1 Tbsp
Dried red chillies	20
Coriander seeds	1 Tbsp
Black peppercorns	1 Tbsp
Cardamom	5 pods
Shallots	7, peeled
Curry leaves	2 stalks
Garlic	7 cloves, peeled and chopped
Ginger	1-cm ($^1/_2$-in) knob
Grated coconut	2$^1/_2$ Tbsp
Water	125 ml (4 fl oz / $^1/_2$ cup)

Add the water little by little when blending to get a smooth paste. You may not need to use all the water.

Toast the fennel in a dry wok. Move it around the wok to prevent it from burning. Toast and grind a larger quantity of fennel and store for future use.

Using a mortar and pestle will ensure that the fennel powder is not too fine.

METHOD

- Prepare paste. Heat oil in a wok and fry dried chillies, coriander, peppercorns and cardamom for 5 minutes. Remove and fry shallots, curry leaves, garlic, ginger and grated coconut until shallots brown lightly.

- Put all paste ingredients except water into a blender. Add water bit by bit and blend mixture until very fine.

- Heat oil in a wok. Add curry leaves, then onions. Cook until onions are brown. Add paste and fry until fragrant. Add chicken pieces and stir-fry to coat completely.

- When juices start sizzling, add salt and turmeric powder. Mix well. Add potatoes now if using.

- Cover wok with a lid and allow chicken to cook gently. Remember to stir occasionally. Cook until sauce is reduced and thickened.

- Toast fennel, then grind into a powder using a mortar and pestle. Sprinkle over chicken and serve hot with rice or breads.

CHICKEN TIKKA

This recipe has been adapted so it can be prepared at home even without a tandoor.

INGREDIENTS

Boneless chicken breasts	500 g (1 lb 1¹/₂ oz)

MARINADE

Cream	125 ml (4 fl oz / ¹/₂ cup)
Plain yoghurt	3 Tbsp
Chilli powder	3 tsp
Garam masala	1 tsp
Cumin powder	¹/₂ tsp
Tomato paste	1 tsp
Sweet mango chutney	1 Tbsp
Yellow food colouring	¹/₂ tsp
Salt	to taste
Coriander (cilantro) leaves	1 sprig, minced
Olive oil	125 ml (4 fl oz / ¹/₂ cup)
Cooking oil	
Onions	3, peeled and sliced
Green chillies	3, chopped
Red and yellow capsicums (bell peppers)	1 each, sliced

GARLIC AND GINGER PASTE

Garlic	6 cloves, peeled and chopped
Ginger	2.5-cm (1-in) knob, peeled and chopped

Cut the chicken breast meat into large cubes so it is easier to thread them onto skewers.

A baking tray can be used as a griddle to grill the chicken. Grease it well using a pastry or oil brush.

Sprinkle the onions, chillies and capsicums over the chicken evenly.

METHOD

- Cut chicken breasts into cubes. Wash and drain well. Make sure there is absolutely no water when it is time to marinate the chicken or the flavour will be diluted.

- Combine marinade ingredients and blend. Combine garlic and ginger paste ingredients and blend.

- Combine marinade and garlic and ginger paste, then marinate chicken for about 4 hours. (The addition of oil ensures that the grilled chicken remains moist.)

- Oil a flat pan or griddle and grill chicken in a preheated oven at 180°C (350°F). Grill for about 15 minutes, then turn chicken over and grill the other side for another 15 minutes.

- Sprinkle half the onions, chillies and capsicum slices over chicken, then drizzle olive oil over. Turn chicken over and sprinkle with remaining onions, chillies and capsicums. Grill for another 10 minutes.

- Alternatively, skewer chicken and capsicums using bamboo skewers and grill for about 15 minutes before turning over to grill the other side for another 15 minutes. Serve with rice or bread and a fresh salad.

CHICKEN WITH CHILLI AND CAPSICUMS

This dish uses very few spices but the chicken fully absorbs the flavour of the onions and capsicums. Keep the cooked dish for a day or two and the flavour will intensify. Cut down the number of dried chillies used if you feel it might be too spicy for you.

Cut the capsicums into half, then remove the core and the seeds.

Cut the capsicum halves into slices, then cut into chunky pieces.

Sauté the chilli and garlic paste with the onions and some capsicums until the oil surfaces.

INGREDIENTS

Onions	3, peeled and sliced
Cooking oil	125 ml (4 fl oz / ¹/₂ cup)
Chicken thighs	8, skinned and each cut into 3 portions
Red, yellow and green capsicums (bell peppers)	1 each, cut into chunks
Tomato sauce	4 Tbsp
Garlic	5 cloves, peeled and minced
Salt	to taste
Sugar	1 Tbsp
Cherry tomatoes	10

PASTE

Dried red chillies	20, soaked in hot water to soften, then drained
Garlic	4 cloves, peeled

GARNISH

Spring onions (scallions)
Coriander leaves (cilantro)

METHOD

- Prepare paste. Grind soaked dried chillies and garlic into a paste.

- Sauté onions and some capsicum chunks in a little oil until fragrant. Add paste and fry until oil surfaces.

- Add chicken and mix to coat well with paste.

- Add remaining capsicums, tomato sauce, garlic and salt to taste. Cook over low heat until chicken has absorbed all the flavours.

- Add sugar and cook for another 10 minutes. Add cherry tomatoes and sauté to mix well.

- Dish out and garnish with spring onions and coriander leaves.

EASY CHICKEN TAJINE

A tajine is a deep-glazed earthenware dish with a conical lid used throughout North Africa. Meals cooked using a tajine are usually slow-braised, and are also known as tajines. This recipe, however, does not require a tajine.

Roast the cumin in a dry pan or wok. Roast a larger quantity and store the rest for use in other recipes.

Dried apricots are usually pitted. If not, pit then slice the apricots using a knife.

Place the stewed tomatoes and peeled garlic into a blender and process into a fine paste.

INGREDIENTS

Stewed tomatoes	410 g (14 1/2 oz / 1 1/2 cups)
Garlic	4 cloves, peeled
Meat curry powder	1/2 Tbsp
Cumin powder	1/2 Tbsp, roasted
Kitchen King masala powder	1 tsp (optional)
Black peppercorns	1 tsp
Salt	to taste
Sugar	1 tsp
Boneless chicken meat	400 g (14 1/3 oz), diced
Canned chickpeas	60 g (2 oz / 1 1/2 cups), with brine
Dried apricots	10, sliced
Raisins or sultanas	20 g (2/3 oz / 1/2 cup)

GARNISH

Red, yellow and green
   capsicum (bell pepper)
   cubes
Sliced dried apricots
Chopped coriander leaves
   (cilantro)

METHOD

- Puree stewed tomatoes with garlic. Pour into a saucepan. Bring to a slow boil.

- Add meat curry powder, cumin powder, masala powder, pepper, salt and sugar. Return to the boil, then add chicken, chickpeas, apricots and raisins or sultanas. Simmer until chicken is cooked and tender.

- Taste and adjust seasoning if necessary. Garnish with capsicum cubes, sliced apricots and chopped coriander leaves or as desired. Serve with bread, rice or cous cous.

TANDOORI CHICKEN

Although there are many ingredients to this recipe, it is not difficult to do. You only have to blend the ingredients together and marinate the chicken. The marinated chicken can be kept frozen for up to 2 months.

INGREDIENTS

Chicken breasts, with bone	10, washed and drained
Ghee (*clarified butter*)	60 g (2 oz / ½ cup)
Mango powder (*amchur*)	3 Tbsp (optional)
Coarse chilli powder	2 Tbsp

MARINADE

Shallots	10, peeled
Garlic	6 cloves, peeled
Ginger	2.5-cm (1-in) knob, peeled
Sugar	1 tsp
Salt	1½ tsp
Chilli paste or powder	1½ Tbsp
Tomato paste	1½ Tbsp
Dijon mustard	2 tsp
Plain yoghurt	120 ml (4 fl oz / ½ cup)
Cumin seeds	½ tsp, dry-roasted and finely ground
Garam masala	½ tsp
Saffron	10 strands
Red food colouring	¼ tsp
Mango chutney	2 Tbsp
Lemon juice	2 Tbsp

GARNISH

Lemon wedges
Sliced onions
Coriander leaves (cilantro)

Prick the chicken using a fork or make shallow cuts using a sharp knife. This will allow the flavour of the marinade to penetrate the chicken.

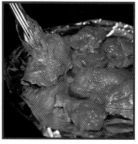

Arrange the chicken apart on a lined baking tray so they will cook more evenly.

Sprinkle the mango and chilli powder over the chicken using your fingers to distribute it more evenly.

METHOD

- Combine and grind ingredients for marinade.

- Pat chicken dry with absorbent paper. Prick chicken or make shallow cuts to allow marinade to penetrate. Rub marinade into meat thoroughly. Cover and refrigerate for at least 1 hour.

- Preheat oven to 200°C (400°F).

- Place chicken on a tray lined with greaseproof paper or aluminium foil and bake for 30 minutes until done.

- Sprinkle half the ghee, mango and chilli powders all over chicken. Turn chicken over and sprinkle the remaining ghee, mango and chilli powders over. Bake for another 15 minutes.

- Serve chicken with a lemon wedges, sliced onions and coriander leaves.

MEAT

Chilli Sausage on Creamy Potato Mash

Fiery Pork Curry

Creamy Mutton Stew (Mutton *Ishtew*)

Mutton Pepper Fry

Indian Shepherd's Pie

CHILLI SAUSAGE ON CREAMY POTATO MASH

This easy-to-prepare dish is comfort food at its best.

Cut the rashers of bacon into small pieces.

Caramelise the onions over medium-low heat to prevent them from burning. The onions will soften and brown as they caramelise.

Mix the milk well into the mashed potatoes using a potato masher.

INGREDIENTS

Garlic	5 cloves, peeled and minced
Onion	1, peeled and minced
Olive oil	
Streaky bacon	4 rashers, chopped into small pieces
Canned kidney beans	450 g (1 lb / 2 cups), reserve can for use later
Water	
Chilli powder	2 tsp
Roasted cumin powder	1 tsp
Ground black pepper	1 tsp
Salt	to taste
Condensed tomato soup	250 g (9 oz)
Fat, juicy sausages	6, scored
Potatoes	4, boiled in skins until soft, then peeled
Butter	2 tsp
Salt	to taste
Black peppercorns	1 Tbsp, crushed
Milk	180 ml (6 fl oz / $^3/_4$ cup)

GARNISH

Onions	2, peeled and thinly sliced
Coriander leaves (cilantro)	1 sprig, chopped

METHOD

- In a saucepan, sauté minced garlic and onion in 1 Tbsp olive oil until golden brown. Add bacon and fry until slightly crisp. Add kidney beans. Fill empty kidney beans can with water and set aside.

- Add chilli and cumin powders, pepper and salt. Mix well, then pour in tomato soup. Mix, then add water from kidney beans can. Simmer over low heat. Meanwhile, slow cook sausages with 1 tsp olive oil until skin is crisp.

- Put sausages into the pot with kidney beans and cook for another 15 minutes. Add some chopped coriander leaves. Caramelise onions in a pan and set aside for garnishing.

- Mash potatoes while still hot. Add butter, salt and pepper. Add milk and mix until creamy and light. Add half the fried onions and remaining coriander leaves to mash and mix. Serve sausages and beans topped with caramelised onions and coriander. Serve with mash.

FIERY PORK CURRY

This recipe is best eaten with piping hot, soft idlis. It is a very spicy dish, so reduce the amount of dried red chillies used according to taste.

Use pork that has some fat content so the final dish will not be too hard or dry. Cut it up into small, bite-sized pieces with a sharp knife.

Combine pork and spices and leave for 30 minutes to marinate pork.

To test if the pork is tender, use a fork. The fork should pierce through the pork easily.

INGREDIENTS

Pork, with some fat	500 g (1 lb 1 1/2 oz), diced
Onions	2, peeled and cut into chunks
Green chillies	3, sliced
Ginger	2.5-cm (1-in) knob, peeled and sliced
Garlic	5 cloves, peeled and sliced
Cinnamon	1 stick
Cardamom	5 pods
Cloves	5
Salt	1 tsp
Vinegar	1 Tbsp
Cooking oil	1 1/2 Tbsp
Bay leaves	3
Water	250 ml (8 fl oz / 1 cup)
Curry leaves	2 stalks

PASTE

Dried red chillies	20
Coriander	1 Tbsp
Black pepper peppercorns	1/2 Tbsp
Cumin seeds	1/2 Tbsp
Water	125ml (4 fl oz / 1/2 cup)

METHOD

- Prepare paste. In a dry wok, roast dried red chillies until smoky but not burnt. Remove and roast coriander seeds, pepper and cumin briefly until seeds are hot. While still hot, grind spices with roasted chillies and water until very fine.

- Mix pork with ground paste, onions, chillies, ginger, garlic, cinnamon, cardamom, cloves, salt, vinegar, oil and bay leaves. Set aside for 30 minutes.

- Add water and mix well. Cook over medium heat until water begins to boil. Reduce heat to low and simmer for 30 minutes, stirring occasionally.

- Test meat and if tender, adjust seasoning to taste. Plunge curry leaves in and set aside for another 30 minutes before serving with rice.

CREAMY MUTTON STEW
(MUTTON ISHTEW)

This dish goes well with Indian breads such as appoms and dosas or crusty French bread.

INGREDIENTS

Potatoes	6, halved and boiled in their skins
Onions	2, peeled and sliced
Green chillies	5, split in half lengthwise
Ginger	2.5-cm (1-in) knob, peeled and sliced
Curry leaves	4 stalks
Mutton	300 g (11 oz), diced and boiled until tender; reserve stock
Salt	to taste
Coconut milk	125 ml (4 fl oz / $^1/_2$ cup)
Fresh milk	125 ml (4 fl oz / $^1/_2$ cup)
Cooking oil	1 Tbsp
Ground white pepper	1–2 tsp

METHOD

- Peel and mash potatoes. Place in a pan and add enough water to cover.

- Add onions, green chillies, ginger and 2 stalks of curry leaves. Bring to a slow boil and stir to mix.

- Add cooked mutton and stock. Add salt and stir in coconut milk and fresh milk. Cook for 15 minutes.

- Put in remaining curry leaves, drizzle in oil and swirl the pot to mix. Add pepper to taste.

- Set aside for at least 30 minutes before serving with bread.

Split the green chillies in half lengthwise using a small knife.

Peel the skin off the boiled potatoes using a knife to ease it off. The skin will peel off quite easily.

Swirl the pot to mix the ingredients. Use kitchen towels or oven gloves when handling hot utensils.

MUTTON PEPPER FRY

This dish is fragrant with the aroma of freshly ground black pepper. Adjust the amount of black pepper to taste as desired.

Season the mutton with the paste. Knead it into the mutton using hands for the best results. Wear gloves as necessary.

Add just enough water to cover the mutton. Using too much water will cause the stock to be diluted and too little water will cause the final dish to be dry.

Stir-fry the dried red chillies in the hot oil until they brown. Do this in a well-ventilated area as the fumes from the chillies can be overpowering.

INGREDIENTS

Mutton	1.5 kg (3 lb 4$^1/_2$ oz), cut into small cubes
Water	
Cooking oil	6 Tbsp
Mustard seeds	2 tsp
Curry leaves	3 stalks
Urad dhal	3 Tbsp
Dried red chillies	3
Shallots	500 g (1 lb 1$^1/_2$ oz), peeled and sliced
Chilli powder	3 Tbsp
Tomato paste	1$^1/_2$ Tbsp
Dark soy sauce	2 Tbsp (optional)
Freshly ground black pepper	1 Tbsp
Salt	to taste
Sugar	$^1/_2$ tsp

PASTE

Garlic	10 cloves, peeled
Ginger	2.5-cm (1-in) knob, peeled
Salt	to taste

METHOD

- Prepare paste. Combine garlic, ginger and salt and grind into a paste.

- Rub paste into mutton and leave for 30 minutes.

- Place mutton in a pot, then add enough water to cover mutton. Bring to the boil for 20 minutes, stirring.

- Heat oil in a wok and stir-fry dried red chillies. When chillies brown, add mustard seeds, curry leaves, urad dhal and sliced shallots. Fry until shallots are soft.

- Add boiled mutton and stock, chilli powder, tomato paste, soy sauce and pepper. Stir well. Add salt and sugar.

- Cover and cook over medium heat, stirring occasionally, until meat is tender.

- Serve with rice, chapatti or plain crusty bread.

INDIAN SHEPHERD'S PIE

The use of chilli powder in this version of shepherd's pie makes it lightly spicy.

Sauté the minced meat until the colour changes to indicate that it is cooked. Use the spatula to break up the clumps of meat.

Sauté the filling until it is almost dry. This will ensure that the final dish is not too soggy.

Sprinkle the cheese over the layer of mashed potatoes evenly.

INGREDIENTS

FILLING

Cooking oil	
Onion	1, peeled and minced
Garlic	5 cloves, peeled and minced
Meat (mutton or lamb)	500 g (1 lb 1^1/$_2$ oz), minced
Canned stewed tomatoes	1 can, 410 g (14^1/$_2$ oz)
Chilli powder	1 Tbsp
Cumin powder	1 tsp, roasted
Freshly ground black pepper	1 Tbsp
Tomato paste	1 Tbsp
Coriander leaves (cilantro)	25 g (1 oz / ^{1}/$_2$ cup), chopped
Salt	to taste

TOPPING

Potatoes	6–7, boiled in skins until soft then peeled
Fresh milk	125 ml (4 fl oz / ^{1}/$_2$ cup)
Salt	to taste
Ground black pepper	to taste
Cheddar cheese	50 g (2 oz / ^{1}/$_2$ cup), grated
Mozzarella	50 g (2 oz / ^{1}/$_2$ cup), grated
Bread crumbs	50 g (2 oz / ^{1}/$_2$ cup)
Carrots	50 g (2 oz / 1 cup), peeled and shredded
Coriander leaves (cilantro)	25 g (1 oz / ^{1}/$_2$ cup), minced

METHOD

- Heat some oil and sauté onions and garlic until fragrant. Add meat and cook until colour changes.

- Add all remaining filling ingredients and mix well. Cook until meat is done and liquid has almost dried up.

- Roughly mash potatoes and mix in milk, salt and pepper.

- Spoon meat into an ovenproof dish and level it out. Top with mashed potatoes, then sprinkle bread crumbs, carrots, coriander leaves and cheeses over.

- Bake in a preheated oven at 180°C (350°F) until top is golden brown. Remove from oven and leave to cool slightly before serving.

DESSERTS

Cream of Jackfruit and Sago (Chakka Prathaman)

Date Pudding with Vanilla Custard

Green Mung Payasam

Indian Bread and Butter Pudding

Steamed Jackfruit Turnover (*Ada*)

CREAM OF JACKFRUIT AND SAGO (CHAKKA PRATHAMAN)

In Kerala, the jackfruit is a most versatile fruit. Young jackfruit is used in savoury dishes while ripe jackfruit is made into jam or used in desserts like this one.

Cut the jackfruit into thin strips, then cut across the strips to get small dices.

Obtain fresh coconut flesh and cut it into slivers.

Fry the coconut slivers and cashew nuts in the hot ghee until they turn golden brown in colour. Drain on absorbent paper.

INGREDIENTS

Jackfruit	1 kg (2 lb 3 oz), stones discarded
Sago	30 g (1 oz / ¼ cup), soak for 20 minutes, then drained
Water	700 ml (23 fl oz / 3 cups)
Salt	¼ tsp
Dark brown sugar	480 g (17 oz / 2 cups)
Coconut milk	500 ml (16 fl oz / 2 cups)
Ghee	½ Tbsp
Cardamom	10 pods, pounded into powder

GARNISH

Ghee (clarified butter)	2 tsp
Fresh coconut slivers*	114 g (4 oz / ¼ cup)
Cashew nuts	10, chopped

METHOD

- Dice jackfruit and place in a saucepan with sago. Add water to cover jackfruit and sago completely. Bring to the boil, then reduce to moderate heat.

- When jackfruit is soft, add salt and brown sugar. Cook for 10 minutes until jackfruit has absorbed the flavour of the molasses. Stir in powdered cardamom.

- Carefully pour in coconut milk and simmer gently. Add ghee and simmer for 20 minutes for flavours to infuse.

- Meanwhile, prepare garnish. Heat ghee, then add coconut and cashew nuts. Fry to a golden brown. Drain and use to garnish cream of jackfruit.

- Serve hot or chilled.

DATE PUDDING WITH BUTTERSCOTCH TOPPING

This recipe might seem like a lot of work, but it is really simple and when you finally get the chance to dig in, it will all be worth it.

INGREDIENTS

PUDDING

Boiling water	300 ml (10 fl oz / 1¼ cups)
Seedless dates	170 g (6 oz), chopped
Bicarbonate of soda	1 tsp
Butter	110 g (4 oz), at room temperature
Brown sugar	170 g (6 oz / ¾ cup)
Eggs	2
Self-raising flour	170 g (6 oz / 1½ cups), sifted
Vanilla essence	½ tsp
Chopped nuts (optional)	

BUTTERSCOTCH TOPPING

Brown sugar	200 g (7 oz / 1 cup)
Cream	300 ml (10 fl oz / 1¼ cups)
Butter	180 g (6½ oz)

Pour the boiling water over the dates to soften them.

Cream the butter and sugar with an electric cake mixer until light and fluffy.

Heat the brown sugar, cream and butter over low heat until sugar and butter are completed melted. Stir continously to prevent the sugar from burning.

METHOD

- Preheat the oven to 180°C (350°F). Grease an 18-cm (7-in) square cake tin.

- Prepare pudding. Pour boiling water over dates, sprinkle in bicarbonate of soda and leave to cool. When cool, blend into a paste.

- Cream butter and sugar until fluffy. Add eggs one at a time, ensuring that egg is fully incorporated before adding the next one.

- Fold in flour and stir in date mixture and vanilla essence. Pour into cake tin and bake for 30–40 minutes or until a knife inserted into the centre of cake comes out clean. Set aside to cool.

- Combine ingredients for butterscotch topping and cook over low heat to melt sugar and butter.

- Serve pudding with butterscotch topping and sprinkle nuts over as desired.

GREEN MUNG PAYASAM

Payasams are sweet desserts served after an Indian meal.

INGREDIENTS

Green mung beans	100 g (3¹/₂ oz / ²/₃ cup), soaked overnight and drained
Water	2 litres (64 fl oz / 8 cups)
Sago pearls	30 g (1 oz / ¹/₄ cup), soaked in cold water for 20–30 minutes, then drained
Brown sugar	300 g (11 oz / 1¹/₃ cups)
Coconut milk	300 ml (10 fl oz / 1¹/₂ cups)
Cardamom	10 pods, ground and sifted
Salt	2 tsp

METHOD

- Cook beans in water until beans are soft but not mushy. Drain beans and reserve water.

- Pour cooked beans into a saucepan. Add brown sugar and stir well. Cook over medium heat for 10 minutes, then add 250 ml (8 fl oz / 1 cup) reserved liquid from boiling beans. Top up with water if necessary to cover beans. Continue to cook over medium heat to allow beans to absorb the flavour of the brown sugar.

- Add drained sago and more water if necessary to cover beans. Continue to cook until sago is translucent.

- Add salt, then coconut milk and cardamom powder. Simmer over low heat until payasam is thick, stirring occasionally to keep sago from sticking to the bottom of the pan.

- Serve hot or chilled, with a little dollop of coconut cream (optional).

Pound the cardamom pods into powder using a mortar and pestle.

When the sago is cooked, it will start to float and become translucent.

Cook the payasam until it is about the thickness of custard.

INDIAN BREAD AND BUTTER PUDDING

This sweet, creamy dessert is a great way to use up leftover bread, and will delight both children and adults alike.

Line a baking or casserole dish with the bread slices and ensure that they overlap and cover the base of the dish.

Pour the custard evenly over the bread and peaches so they are well coated.

Sprinkle the crushed nuts over the pudding evenly.

INGREDIENTS

Sliced bread	300 g (11 oz)
Butter	
Peach syrup (from canned peaches)	125 ml (2 fl oz / $1/2$ cup)
Canned peaches	250 g (9 oz), drained weight, sliced

CUSTARD

Eggs	3
Sugar	150 g ($5^1/3$ oz)
Milk	300 ml (10 fl oz / $1^1/4$ cups)
Cream	100 ml ($3^1/2$ fl oz / $3/8$ cup)
Cinnamon powder	$1/2$ tsp
Vanilla essence	1 tsp
Crushed nuts	

METHOD

- Butter bread slices and cut in half to get triangles.

- Line a baking or casserole dish with buttered bread slices.

- Drizzle peach syrup over bread and arrange peach slices on top. Set aside.

- Beat eggs lightly with a whisk, then add sugar and whisk until sugar is dissolved.

- Add milk, cream, cinnamon powder and vanilla essence. Whisk to mix well.

- Pour mixture over bread and peaches. Use a spoon to gently press bread down, so bread is covered in mixture. Set aside for 10 minutes.

- Bake in a preheated oven at 180°C (350°F) for 30 minutes. Sprinkle nuts over and serve warm with vanilla ice cream.

STEAMED JACKFRUIT TURNOVER (ADA)

This simple snack is redolent with the fragrance of jackfruit and coconut, and goes well with coffee and tea.

Combine the ingredients in a wok and cook until the sugar is melted and a jam-like consistency is achieved. Stir continuously to prevent burning.

Combine the ingredients for the batter and keep stirring to mix well until a smooth batter is achieved.

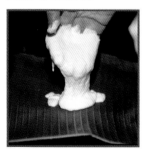

Use your hands or a tablespoon to put a small amount of batter on the banana leaf. Using more batter will increase the cooking time.

INGREDIENTS

Jackfruit	500 g (1 lb 1¹/₂ oz), stones discarded and minced
Grated coconut	300 g (11 oz / 4 cups)
Dark brown sugar	300 g (11 oz / 1¹/₂ cups)
Cardamon powder	1 tsp
Salt	¹/₂ tsp
Water	125 ml (4 fl oz / ¹/₂ cup)
Banana leaves	
Batter	
Plain (all-purpose) flour	500 g (1 lb 1¹/₂ oz / 5 cups), sifted
Water	300 ml (10 fl oz / 1¹/₄ cups)
Salt	a pinch
Ghee (clarified butter)	1 Tbsp

METHOD

- Cook jackfruit, grated coconut, dark brown sugar, cardamon powder, salt and water in a wok over medium heat until mixture is thick with a jam-like consistency.

- Prepare batter. Combine flour, water and salt to get a thick batter. Add ghee and mix until smooth. Leave for 10 minutes.

- Place some batter on a banana leaf and spread it out over the centre of the leaf. Place a generous spoonful of jackfruit jam on batter, then fold leaf over and place in a steamer for about 10 minutes. Repeat until ingredients are used up.

- Unwrap and serve hot or cold.

GLOSSARY
& INDEX

GLOSSARY

AJWAIN

Besides being used as a spice for cooking, ajwain is also known for its medicinal properties. These tiny little seeds are infused in water and used as home remedies for colic, diarrhoea and indigestion. Ajwain has a sharp taste and is frequently used in the preparation of crispy snacks like muruku.

ASAFOETIDA

This is dried gum resin that adds an unmatchable, exotic flavour to dishes. It is available in two forms—powder and its original sticky form that has to broken up into pieces on a grinding stone or cut up with a sharp knife. It is best known as the flatulence reliever and, as such, is always added to recipes using lentils or dhals.

CARDAMOM

Inside the cardamom pod are tiny, brown aromatic seeds. The pods are usually added whole to dishes for flavour as without the pods, the seeds are very pungent. In Indian cooking, cardamom is used in making garam masala and other curry powders.

CHANA DHAL

Chana dhal is yellow in colour and looks somewhat like split peas. It is used in Indian curries and can also be ground into flour to make the batter for a number of Indian breads.

CORIANDER

Although not really seeds, these tiny fruit are commonly referred to as seeds to distinguish them from coriander leaves (cilantro) in recipes. In Indian cooking, both the fresh coriander leaves and seeds are used. When lightly roasted, the seeds impart a lovely flavour and aroma to vegetables and meat curries. However, use sparingly and roast lightly or the finished dish will have a bitter aftertaste.

COTTAGE CHEESE (*PANEER*)

Cottage cheese has the ability to absorb the flavours of the sauces that it has been cooked in. To make cottage cheese, bring 3 litres (96 fl oz / 12 cups) milk to the boil. Stir occasionally until it comes to a slow boil. Add 6 Tbsp lemon juice. The milk will curdle and separate from the whey. Strain using a muslin cloth bag and hang the curdled milk up to allow the whey to drain completely. Squeeze out any remaining water and roll the whey into a ball. Place a weight, such as a mortar, on it and keep aside for a couple of hours. Remove the cloth to reveal chalk-white cottage cheese.

CUMIN

Cumin seeds or jeera is usually added to the hot oil at the start of the cooking so that the oil is infused with its flavour. It is also dry-roasted and ground, then sprinkled on yoghurt, snacks and salads. When roasting and grinding cumin seeds, it is best to roast and store just a little at a time as the ground cumin loses its fragrance easily. Warm cumin water is said to be a great digestive after a spicy meal.

DRIED FENUGREEK (METHI) LEAVES

Dried fenugreek leaves are more commonly used in North Indian cooking than South Indian cooking. They have a smoky aroma and are used to add flavour to curries. Dried fenugreek leaves are sold packaged in small boxes.

CURRY LEAVES

Curry leaves are very fragrant. They are commonly added to oil for tempering, used as garnish, chopped and added to salads, yoghurt or lassi or thinly sliced and added to meat cutlets, patties and omelettes.

DRIED RED CHILLIES

These come in different sizes and varying strengths of spiciness. The long crinkled ones are not as hot as the short, smooth ones. I usually buy the crinkled ones and add a few extra fresh chillies to get a good spicy chilli paste. Dried red chillies need to be soaked in hot water to soften, then blended with a little water into a smooth paste. Add a dash of salt, mix and store in the refrigerator.

FENUGREEK SEEDS

This is another spice that is as ancient and as integral a part of Indian cooking as turmeric. Fenugreek seeds have a very bitter taste and a most unique smell. Just a pinch makes a difference to fish curries and yoghurt-based dishes. Fenugreek seeds also have medicinal properties. For an upset stomach, stir the seeds in a cup of boiling water and strain before drinking.

FENNEL SEEDS

Fennel seeds are often confused with cumin seeds because they look somewhat similar. Fennel seeds are slightly bigger and greenish in colour while cumin is brown. Fennel is also sweeter and is often eaten after a meal as a breath freshener. Roast fennel in a dry pan, grind into a powder and sprinkle on meat dishes just before dishing out for additional fragrance.

GRATED COCONUT

This is the grated flesh of coconut. It can be used in cooking in this grated form or squeezed for its fragrant, creamy white milk. Grind grated coconut with a pinch of cumin, a clove of garlic or some cashewnuts before stirring into curries for a smooth, tasty sauce. You can also use grated coconut as a garnish to a stir-fried vegetable dish.

MUSTARD SEEDS

These tiny black seeds are an essential spice in South Indian cooking. A curry is simply not done unless you have tempered it with a dose of hot oil, mustard seeds, curry leaves and sometimes a dried red chilli. Mustard seeds have a slightly bitter aftertaste and this quality makes them perfect for adding to pickles.

PUMPKIN

The pumpkins used in this book are small, with greenish skin and orange flesh. In Indian cooking, pumpkins are used in chutneys and curries, but they are also great for baking, barbequing or roasting.

JACKFRUIT

This large oblong tropical fruit has spiny skin. When opening a ripe jackfruit, oil the knife to prevent the sap from sticking. Inside, the flesh is golden yellow in colour. Raw jackfruit makes delicious side dishes and ripe ones make good jams, payasams and ada. Some people are put off by the smell of jackfruit, such as they are by durains.

RIDGE GOURD

Like the snake gourd, this is a simple vegetable that is popular in Asia despite its mild taste. When selecting ridge gourd, make sure it is green and fresh. If there is a hollow feel about it, leave it, as it can be dry and bitter after cooking.

SAGO

These opaque white balls are made from starch extracted from the sago palm. Sago is commonly used in desserts and sweets. Cooking sago can be tricky. The first thing to remember is that a little sago goes a long way meaning that it doubles in volume as it cooks. So always use a fairly large container. Wash well and cover completely with water, then bring to the boil slowly. Stir and make sure there is enough water or the sago will stick to the bottom of the pot and burn. When the white sago balls turn translucent, the sago is done.

SNAKE GOURD

This long, thin vegetable is perfect with dhals. It has a subtle flavour and needs boosting with chillies, curry powders and onions. Peel off the skin using a vegetable peeler before use.

SWEET POTATO

Also known as kumara, this simple root vegetable can be used in starters, main courses, desserts or even as a garnish. Choose sweet potatoes that have orange coloured flesh as these have a wonderful flavour.

TAMARIND PULP

This is an essential ingredient in South Indian cooking, especially in dishes that require a tangy flavour like fish curries. Tamarind pulp is available in most Asian stores. To use, take a 2-cm (1-in) ball of pulp and soak in warm water for a few minutes. Knead the soaked pulped with your fingers to break it up and loosen the seeds. Strain and use as required.

TORCH GINGER BUD

As its name suggests, this plant belongs to the ginger family. The tightly closed buds are light pink in colour and have a sweet, tangy fragrance. Shave or thinly slice the bud and add it to salads for both colour and flavour.

WINTER MELON

Winter melons have powdery green skin and snowy white flesh. These melons are special to the Indians as they believe that it is auspicious. As such, winter melons can usually be seen at Indian weddings, housewarming ceremonies and also ceremonies for the blessing of babies. In cooking, winter melons are used in curries and also made into sweet strips that are sometimes used in cakes. In North India, a popular sweet made of winter melon is petha.

TURMERIC

This is one of the most ancient and most important spices in Indian cooking. It is used extensively in the preparation of curries, pickles and marinades. The rhizome is also often ground into a powder and used to spice and colour foods.

URAD DHAL

This dried lentil is used to ferment batter when making Indian breads such as idlis, dosas and vadais. When making batters of this sort, skinned urad dhal is used so the dosas and idlis will be light in colour.

VARK

This is made from real silver. It is an airy, soft tissue which is used to decorate Indian desserts and sweets. It comes wrapped in greaseproof paper. Keep in an airtight container.

INDEX